My Hospital Experience

by

Rev. Bud Robinson

First Fruits Press
Wilmore, Kentucky
2014

My Hospital Experience by Bud Robinson

Published by First Fruits Press, © 2014
Previously Published by Pentecostal Publishing Company [191-?]

ISBN: 9781621711629 (print), 9781621711612 (digital)

Digital version at
http://place.asburyseminary.edu/firstfruitsheritagematerial/79/

First Fruits Press is a digital imprint of the Asbury Theological Seminary, B.L. Fisher Library. Asbury Theological Seminary is the legal owner of the material previously published by the Pentecostal Publishing Co. and reserves the right to release new editions of this material as well as new material produced by Asbury Theological Seminary. Its publications are available for noncommercial and educational uses, such as research, teaching and private study. First Fruits Press has licensed the digital version of this work under the Creative Commons Attribution Noncommercial 3.0 United States License. To view a copy of this license, visit http://creativecommons.org/licenses/by-nc/3.0/us/.

For all other uses, contact First Fruits Press

Robinson, Bud, 1860-1942.
   My hospital experience / by Bud Robinson.
   32 pages ; 21 cm.
   Wilmore, Ky. : First Fruits Press, ©2014.
   Reprint. Previously published: Louisville, KY : Pentecostal Publishing Company, [191-?].
   ISBN: 9781621711629 (pbk.)
   1. Robinson, Bud, 1860-1942. 2. Church of the Nazarene -- Clergy -- Biography. I. Title.
BX8699.N38 R62 2014   289.9

Cover design by Wes Wilcox

First Fruits Press
The Academic Open Press of Asbury Theological Seminary
204 N. Lexington Ave., Wilmore, KY 40390
859-858-2236
first.fruits@asburyseminary.edu
asbury.to/firstfruits

My Hospital Experience

Rev. Bud Robinson

Price 25 cents.

PENTECOSTAL PUBLISHING COMPANY
Louisville, Kentucky.

MY HOSPITAL EXPERIENCE

To my many friends scattered over this land who have sent in requests for me to put my hospital experience in booklet form:

After praying over it and studying the question for several months, I have finally decided to put this wonderful experience in the form of a book in order that my friends may see the dealings of the Lord with me.

Before I take up the experience itself I want to give you a few scriptures that, to me, were never understood until after I went through this fearful ordeal of suffering. We find in Paul's letter to the Romans, the eighth chapter and twenty-eighth verse, this very peculiar statement: "And we know that all things work together for good to them that love God, to them who are called according to His purpose."

This scripture was to me more of a mystery than anything else until I put in five months and a half on my back. And again I read in Revelation 2:10 this very peculiar statement: "Fear none of those things which thou shalt suffer: behold, the devil shall cast some of you into prison that ye may be tried." And then again, we notice in 1st Peter 4:12, these remarkable words: "Beloved, think it not strange concerning the fiery trial which is to try you as though some strange thing happened unto you." Then we read in the 15th and 16th verses, "But let none of you suffer as a murderer or as a thief, or as an evil-doer, or as a busy-body in other men's matters, yet if any man suffer as a Christian, let him not be ashamed, but let him glorify God on this behalf. Wherefore, let them that suffer according to the will of God, commit the

MY HOSPITAL EXPERIENCE

keeping of their souls to Him in well doing as unto a faithful Creator."

Again we will read a few verses from the 11th chapter of 2nd Corinthians. I want to read this because of the fact that some people seem to believe that it would have been impossible for me to be smashed up by an automobile and lay on my back for months unless I had been a backslider and altogether out of the will of God. But no Bible reader will believe for one moment that St. Paul was a backslider when he suffered the things that are described in the 11th chapter of 2nd Corinthians.

We will read from the 24th to the 28th verses: "Of the Jews five times received I forty stripes save one; thrice was I beaten with rods; once was I stoned, thrice I suffered ship-wreck, a night and a day I have been in the deep; in journeyings often, in perils of waters, in perils of robbers, in perils by mine own countrymen, in perils by the heathen, in perils in the city, in perils in the wilderness, in perils in the sea, in perils among false brethren; in weariness and painfulness, in watchings often, in hunger and in thirst, in fasting often, in cold and nakedness; besides those things that are without, that which cometh upon me daily, the care of all the churches."

Any reader will see here that no mortal man could have endured the real suffering that the Apostle Paul endured unless he had been sustained by Divine grace, and no God-loving man can believe that St. Paul had to suffer all these fearful things in order to keep him religious, or to restore him from a state of backsliding. And now one other text will lead me up to my hospital experience. We now read in Philippians 1:12. Brother Will Huff called my attention to this verse of scripture after I was able to go back to work. I want the reader to notice the reading of this verse: "But I would ye should understand brethren, that the things which happened unto me, have fallen out rather unto the furtherance of the gospel."

Here, the reader will notice that St. Paul declares emphatically that the things which happened unto him, had fallen out rather unto the furtherance of the gospel. That is, by his suffering and fearful hardship, the gospel of Jesus Christ was made to grow and flourish and prosper. If I didn't think that God allowed me to be smashed up in order that I could be a greater blessing to the world, I would never put this story in print, and as far as I am able to judge myself, I was in as good a condition, spiritually and physically, to be smashed up as a man could be.

I had prayed and fasted for thirty hours when I was smashed up. A peculiar, strange feeling had settled down over me that something that I didn't understand and couldn't see through, and couldn't tell what it was, was to take place in my life. I had prayed and fasted over the last day of May and come down to June 1st, which was the Holy Sabbath day of 1919. I didn't desire anything to eat, and early Sunday morning I went to prayer and talked with God until eleven o'clock, and went to church and God gave us a beautiful service, the Rev. C. E. Cornell preaching.

After the morning service I wanted nothing to eat, but went to my room and got on my knees and stayed there until two-thirty. I arose from my knees and went to church and preached on the subject of Scriptural Holiness. My heart was overflowing with the love of Jesus, but my friends seemed to think I must be sick or something ailed me. Bro. Cornell asked me if I was sick, and I told him I was not. He asked me if I had heard any bad news anyway, and I told him, "none in the world." But after the service was over I went back to my room and got on my knees and went to prayer. Such a strange feeling came over me, that I was afraid to go to church, but I told the Lord that I was His man and if I was going to die or anything was going to happen to me He knew I was His man from my hat to my heels, and if I died on my way to church I would get into heaven before my heels got cold. I walked up to church and Bro. Cornell preached a beautiful sermon that night, and we had a large crowd at the altar ,and I stayed and helped to pray them through until ten o'clock. It was only about three blocks to my room, and I left the church and walked down to the corner of 16th and Valancia Ave., and the strangest feeling I ever had in my life seemed to settle down over me and I stood on the street corner and looked up at the stars and wept aloud. And I asked the Lord to do a certain thing for me, and I asked the Lord to not allow a certain thing to take place in my life, but God knew my life better than I knew myself, and no doubt He could see that the thing which was troubling me, would in the long run work out for me a far more exceeding and eternal weight of glory. When I asked the Lord to not allow a certain thing to take place, I started across the street and got hemmed in between two automobiles and a street car and one of them was bound to get me. I gave a leap and jumped from in front of one car and lit on the street car track. To my surprise the street car was on my right and was so close to me that I could have touched it with my hand, and I knew if that big steel car ran over me I would be crushed in a moment, and as I leaped from the street car track, a large automobile was trying to outrun the street car, and I saw that it was bound to strike me, and as I struck the ground the big car struck me. I heard the awful crash and felt the pain shoot through my body and heard the bones cracking. The men that were on the sidewalk said I shot into the air, they thought, ten feet high, and I fell thirty feet in front of where the big car struck me. The only time I lost my consciousness was while I was going through the air. I knew when I struck the ground. I heard some more bones pop, but by the time I had struck the ground the big car had come on and run over me, and as all the wheels of the big car ran over my body I heard some more bones pop.

The man stopped the car and he and his wife jumped out, and she said, "Oh, we have killed you." I said to her, "Sister, I am not dead." She said, "No, but you are dying, and will be dead in a few minutes." I told her that I felt like I was in heaven, but I didn't think I was dying. But she seemed to be perfectly convinced that I would be dead in a few minutes. Her husband, by that time, tried to raise me up. I loved him with such love that I am sure it was the same kind of love that Jesus had for me when He hung on the cross. I tried to put my arms around him and hug him, but my arms were broken all to pieces and I couldn't move either one of them. By that time a big policeman ran across the street and swore. I spoke to him and told him to not swear, that I was a minister and didn't want to hear him swear. He raised his club and I thought was going to hit the man that had run me down, and I spoke to him and told him not to do it. He then went to arrest him, and I wouldn't allow him to do that. I told him the man was not to blame, and he said, "Don't you want me to arrest the man that has killed you?" and I told him, "No, that the man was not to blame." I was still lying on the street then and had not been picked up. And in his excitement the policeman grabbed me by the left arm and almost pulled my arm off, until it was the worst bruised arm I have ever seen.

And now to try to tell of my smash-up would be almost impossible. My left arm was pulled bottom-upwards, and the bone broken about an inch and a half below the joints, and the bone running down to the elbow was split. My right arm was broken just below the shoulder, and so badly slivered that a number of pieces of the bone went out into the muscle, and the long end of the bone was driven right through the muscle and through the undershirt sleeve and top shirt sleeve and coat sleeve, and the end of the bone came on over and struck through my coat into my chest, and when I reached the Emergency there were two inches of the arm bone sticking out through the flesh and my clothes. My left knee was smashed and my left leg was broken, and my left ankle was pulled apart and the foot turned around in the joint.

There is no way to describe the real suffering that

MY HOSPITAL EXPERIENCE

I endured, but the policeman and the man that had smashed me put me into the man's car and drove me to the Emergency. We got there between ten and eleven o'clock in the night, and they received me, but they handled me as though I had been cordwood. I begged for mercy and plead with them to handle me with more ease, but the young men laughed and joked and smoked cigarettes and blew the smoke in my face, and apparently had no more concern for my awful suffering than if I had been a slaughtered pig. One of them, as he cut off my clothes, said to me, "Cap, you're a mighty old man to be smashed up like this." He said, "Are you about seventy years old?" I said, "No, I am about fifty-nine." "Well," he said, "Cap, what's your business, what do you work at?" I told him I was a preacher of the gospel and had been preaching for thirty-nine years. He said, "Well, Cap, all the patience you have preached to the people for thirty-nine years, you are going to need yourself before you get out of the hospital." I found out that he knew pretty well what he was talking about, by the time I left the hospital. But that one night spent in the Emergency in San Francisco, will stand out in my mind the rest of my life, as one of the most horrible nights I have ever spent. I tried to get them a number of times to send for Bro. Cornell and Bros. Smith and Corlett, but they didn't notify them and get them there until between one and two o'clock in the morning, and then Bro. Cornell wired my family, also *The Christian Witness, The Pentecostal Herald, The Herald of Holiness,* and *The Revivalist,* asking the people to pray especially for me, that I had been smashed with an automobile and was in a dangerous condition. And let me say right here, that it was the prayers of God's faithful children in this land that enabled me to pull through and come out again a well man. But God gave me some opportunities to testify to Him that I could never have had if I had not been smashed.

After I had suffered death during the night at the Emergency, at day break a Catholic priest came in and went to the various cots and dug up confessions from the men that were lying all around me. They confessed many things some of them enough, it seemed to me, to wreck a steamboat. He finally came to me and asked if I had anything to confess. I told him I did, that I had a confession I wanted to make. I then told him that Jesus Christ had saved and sanctified me and filled my heart with the Holy Ghost, glory be to God. He seemed to stagger back toward the door, and finally came back near, and asked me if there was anything else I wanted to confess. I told him there was, that I wanted to confess to him that I had preached the gospel of Jesus Christ for thirty-nine years and that He could save sinners and sanctify believers, and that, bless God! I had seen Him do it. He staggered back to the door, and as he went out he looked back at me and said, "If you need me, let me know," and I said, "Bless God, I will." That was the last glimpse I ever had of the Holy Father.

A little after daylight Brothers Cornell and Smith came to the Emergency and brought with them a fine surgeon, Dr. Rumwell, from the Leland Stanford Hospital. The doctor looked me over and didn't want to take my case. He said the old man was so smashed up that he would rot and die but my friends urged him to take me and do all he could for me, telling him they would stand behind me and see that all the bills were paid. Then he came back to me and told me if he took my case he wanted to know how I had lived. I told him I had preached the gospel for thirty-nine years. But he gave me to understand that he had been raised an infidel and knew nothing about God and took no stock in Christianity. I told him that the Lord had saved me, but he told me that he was raised in an infidel home in Illinois and was sent to Paris, France and educated in the University of Paris, and that they knew nothing about God. I told him that I did, that I knew God had saved me, but he finally said he guessed it was all right, and then he wanted to know of me how I had lived morally. I told him I had never drank in my life, and he said, "That is tremendously in your favor." I told him I hadn't touched tobacco since I was a boy, and he said, "You'll get well." He then tested my blood and said it was as clean as a baby's blood. Then he said, "You'll get well." But he said at the time, "Your right arm will cause you a great deal of suffering and you may lose it; it is in a bad fix, but I'll do my best to save it."

Then with the understanding that he was to take my case, Bros. Cornell and Smith sent for the ambulance to move me to the hospital. I think I suffered the most intense agony while I was being moved from the Emergency to the ambulance. A man picked me up in his arms and my broken bones sticking out through the flesh seemed to grate and creak as he carried me to the ambulance, and I am sure that I would have died before they got me across town if it had not been for Brother Corlett, a fine young preacher and singer, who had returned from the battlefields of France. While he was on the battlefield in Europe, a great machine-gun ball passed through his left thigh just below his hip, and he lay twenty-two hours on the battlefield. He knew what fearful suffering was, and how to sympathize with me. He got down on his knees by me in the ambulance with one hand on my brow, and held the other up and prayed. And in his prayers he would tell the Lord that He must spare my life, that they neded me worse on earth than they did in heaven, and that they simply couldn't give me up, that the Lord must touch me and give me back to them to help them preach holiness. Then he would boost for me, as I never heard a boy boost for a man; he would say, "Brother Bud, you are going to get well, you are in a bad fix, but you will pull through. You are going to get well, for we can't spare you." And then he would offer another earnest prayer that God would touch me and spare my life, and by that precious boy boosting for me across town, we finally pulled into the great hospital, and I was unloaded, and they put me in a beautiful room, 303. There was something strange about my smash-up. In my room in the Crown Hotel the day I was smashed the number was 404, and in the hospital in Frisco, my room was 303, and when I was finally shipped to the Pasadena Hospital my room there was 202. I don't know what these numbers stand for, but the Lord knows, I judge.

They worked on me during the day of Monday the

2nd, and got me ready to operate on Tuesday morning, of June 3rd. I went under the ether at 7:20 in the morning and I came out between 11 and 12 o'clock, but oh, my, my, what a fix I was in! I was lying on my back with my left arm bound up to my side until I couldn't move it, and my right arm in a big caste from my shoulder down to my knuckles, and my left leg was in a caste from my knee clear down over my toes. My right leg was bruised in a number of places to the bone and was as black as my coat, and I couldn't move either arm or my left leg, and could just work my right foot a little bit. Then I found out what the young man at the Emergency meant that I would need all the patience that I had ever preached to the people, for myself. I think I would have died in that hospital if it hadn't been for good doctors and a good nurse, and I think more is due to the good nurse than the good doctor. When it comes to patience and love and tenderness and right down sympathy, there is nobody in the world that is equal to a good nurse. However, some of them, I have heard people say, were not good people, but my nurses were just little angels in human form. May God bless their memory. How many lonely hours they sat by my bed and washed and bathed my wounds. They had to feed me like I was a baby, but the amount of patience and endurance a man needs to pull through such a smash-up as I went through, there is none but our gracious heavenly Father knows, but thank God, He was on hand to give me grace and peace and comfort, and while my body was racked in pain, my soul was on the stretch for the glory land.

At this time I wish to thank the many friends who

sent in flowers, for they came in the greatest quatities I have ever seen. There was money sent in from the various parts of the United States, and day by day for three months the flowers came on. I wouldn't have thought it was so remarkable if the flowers had only been sent for a few days, but when they came day by day and kept it up for three months, and such quantities of the most beautiful flowers that man has ever beheld, it showed that the Lord had a hand in the whole thing. I am surprised that on one occasion it was rumored through the hospital that the reason such quantities of beautiful flowers came to my room, was that I was the president of a great railroad system, and the people seemed to think that the railroad men up and down the land were sending in flowers. I told them that I beat that by far, that instead of me being president of a railroad system, I was a second-blessing holiness preacher, and was preaching that Jesus could save sinners and sanctify believers, and if the people who had me in hand, did not believe He could do it, I still believe that they believed that I believed it. Glory to Jesus! I want it known right now in three worlds that while a man is broken to pieces and is absolutely helpless, that there is not enough devils in the pit or out to keep the Lord from so blessing a man's soul that he can shout the victory in the teeth of the devil in spite of difficulties, hardships, and suffering.

On the second day after my operation, the muscles in my leg began to draw around the broken bones until the suffering was so awful that when the pains would strike me in the leg I would scream as loud as I could, and the pains were so fearful and the muscles would

MY HOSPITAL EXPERIENCE 15

draw until it would lift my leg up off of the bed. When the doctor came in I asked him how long this would last, and he answered, "Anywhere between twelve and twenty-four hours." I told him that if I didn't get relief I would be a dead man. He said, "You would die if you could, but you can't." But I said, "Doctor, it is raising my leg up off of the bed, it is so hard." The doctor said, "Just let that leg rear, and if she wants to climb right up over the headboard of the bed, just let her go up."

At that time the District Assembly of the San Francisco district was in session in the Church of the Nazarene down in the city. I asked my wife to go down to the telephone and call Dr. Goodwin, and have him call the Assembly to prayer, that my leg was killing me. Dr. Goodwin called them to prayer, and I saw the prayers of the saints answered. It was the most remarkable thing I have ever seen, and when I say I saw the prayers answered, I don't just mean that they prayed and I got better. All of that took place, glory to God! but I saw more than that; I actually saw the prayers answered. While they were at prayer down in the Assembly Hall, I saw a stream of liquid gold come down from heaven. It was bigger around than my thumb, and seemed to be a stream of liquid gold poured out in heaven, and it was poured on my leg just above my knee, and the stream went down to my toe and back up over my leg to my knee again, and back down to my toe, and I opened my eyes and the pains were gone, and the pain in that leg never returned. I know this was the prayers of the saints.

MY HOSPITAL EXPERIENCE

In spite of the devil and unbelievers God can still show His children wonderful things that He is doing for them. Bless His Holy Name! Someone told me, who was at the Assembly, that when Dr. Goodwin called them to prayer, that every member of the Assembly got on their knees and prayed as loud as they could whoop, and the beauty of it all to me is that everyone of them prayed through and got the answer that God had undertaken in my case and that my leg would be spared, and right here I want to stop long enough to say, Glory to Jesus, I love Him better than ever before, and from the depth of my soul I want to thank Dr. Goodwin and every member of the Assembly for their earnest prayers in my behalf. There is no way that I can ever express to them the love and gratitude that I feel in my heart for everyone of them. Bless God, they are the aristocracy of the skies. In my case they were sky-openers and fire-pullers, sin-killers, and devil-drivers, and some sweet day I expect to sit down on the bank of the "River of Life" with everyone of them.

While I was in the hospital in Frisco, my expenses were in the hands of the Rev. Donald J. Smith, the pastor of the Church of the Nazarene in San Francisco, and when it comes to right down goodness and manhood to the square inch, Donald J. Smith is the biggest man for his size of any man I think I have ever met in the United States. He received the money that was sent for my expenses and raised money among his own people and the Pacific Coast and paid the bills until, when I left the hospital there was not a charge against me.

MY HOSPITAL EXPERIENCE 17

The reader might be informed here that I was holding meetings for Brother Smith when I was smashed and he and his little wife, Sister Ruth, were love and kindness and sympathy personified. I will never forget their love and kindness while I live on earth, and God will reward them both in heaven.

About the second or third day after my smash-up, while I was near the gates of death, the angels of heaven came one day for me and carried me to heaven. I suppose this would be called a vision or something of that kind by most everybody, yet to me it was as real and as beautiful as it will be when I go up. I was carried to the gates of heaven and no mortal man can describe the scenery of that city. The gates of pearl and jasper walls and golden streets are just as real as the brick and mortar that go to make up the average city of the United States, and heaven is just as real a city as Louisville or Cincinnati, or Chicago, or any other American city. It is the home of God, and I was allowed to go up and go in and see the city. There were millions and multiplied millions of angels, and they were more beautiful than I had ever imagined that an angel could be, but as beautiful as the angels were, they were not so beautiful as the redeemed saints. The saints were so beautiful that no pen nor tongue could describe their beauty. They were whiter than the driven snow. And while I beheld the saints, the great organs of heaven began to play. It was so beautiful that there is not a sinner in the world but what, if he could hear the music of that world, he would give his heart to God right on the spot. After the big organs had played for sometime there were millions and millions of saints gathered around the great white throne and they began to sing in the most beautiful tones of voice that I had ever heard. They sang an old hymn that I hadn't heard for some years, it was "Companionship with Jesus, O, How Sweet!" As they sang it seemed that all heaven rejoiced, and the angels seemed to stand still while the saints sang the beautiful old hymn. And Jesus came out of the great multitude of those shining ones, and stood before me and began to talk with me. It was worth all the suffering that I have ever done. If I had been broken ten times as bad as I was, it would have been worth it all, to have made that trip to heaven and to have had Jesus come and look me over and talk with me. My robe seemed to be whiter than the driven snow, and 1 was allowed to see my own heart. It was whiter than snow, and glittered like snow, mingled with gold or something of that kind; and while Jesus was talking to me, two men who had been the best friends to me that I have most ever had in my life, and the men that stood by me during my awful suffering, and raised the money to pay the bills, came and stood, the one on the one side of me, and the other on the other. It was the Rev. C. E. Cornell, of Pasadena, Calif., and the Rev. A. O. Hendricks, of Los Angeles, Calif. These men were so white and beautiful that the angels looked at them and rejoiced. And strange as it may seem to the reader, that God could show me those two men in heaven standing by me, and they are both alive and each one of them is a faithful pastor. But God allowed me to see them there in their beautiful glorified bodies, and it made me rejoice to think that they stood

MY HOSPITAL EXPERIENCE 19

by me in the presence of Jesus. I can never forget their beautiful shining faces, and Jesus seemed to be so well pleased with them as they stood by me, as He talked with me and smile din my face. I saw another preacher that is still alive, come and stand about fifty feet from me. He looked to be about three feet tall and his face looked dark and troubled, and I wondered what it all could mean, and while I was looking at him, I saw another preacher come and stand by him, and the preacher that came and stood by him looked to be much taller, and had a much finer face and cleaner looking, and looked more like the rest of the saints, and as I looked at him he became taller and more beautiful than he had been, but the one he stood by still looked so troubled in his face, and nobody seemed to say a word to him, until it made my heart sad because it seemed nobody there was glad or rejoicing because he was there. I don't know what these things all mean. God only knows, but after Jesus had talked with me awhile He sent me back to this world to tell the people how He loves them, and wants to save all sinners and sanctify every believer and so purify their hearts that they can come and live with Him forever in His beautiful home, and the angels seemed to gather me up someway and brought me back to this world, and I opened my eyes and I was in room 303, in the big hospital in San Francisco. Just what a vision like that means, it is hard to tell, but God had an object in view in the whole thing, and I was so thankful when I got back, that I could go out to tell the world once more that I had made the trip. While I live and keep my mind, it is my business now to try to tell a dying world and a hungry church that Jesus can do all the Bible says He can do. And I am glad I found out that heaven is a real City. We have got to the place now-a-days in a great many of our larger churches that it is preached from many pulpits that heaven is not a locality but a condition, and hell is not a locality but a mere condition. So if the big preachers are right, when a sinner dies, he has no place to go because hell is not a locality and there is no place of eternal punishment, and also if he is correct when a saint dies he has no place to go, for if heaven and hell are not places of joy and sorrow, then the redeemed saints and sinners also would have no place to go when they leave this world. But thanks be unto Him, that always causeth us to triumph! Heaven is a reality and the home of the soul. I was allowed to go and see the City, and to hear the songs and the music and talk with Jesus and then come back to this world again. And while I had believed that all my life, now it is so real to me, that the Home of Jesus is as real as the home of any of my friends. Bless His name forever!

My readers will remember that I told you in the outset that my doctor told me I would have a great deal of trouble with my right arm, and might lose it, as the muscle in the arm for five inches had to be split open because the bones had slivered and the pieces had gone out into the muscles and some of the pieces were six months in working out. I suffered enough with this arm at any time for six months to have taken it off, but yet my doctors fought the infection and took out pieces of bones and did all in their power to save the arm. You will remember that I told you that my doc-

MY HOSPITAL EXPERIENCE 21

tor in Frisco said he didn't believe in religion, but while he would work on my arm it was so bad that I could not do anything but shout and praise God, and tell the doctor how good I loved him, and wanted him to live close to me in heaven, until I know God talked to his heart and put him under conviction, for he said in the hospital he had a real Christian on his hands, and when asked how he knew it he said that while he dressed the wounds of a number of men they cussed the world by sections, and that while he dressed a bad surgical wound for me, that I shouted all the time, and he knew by that that I was a Christian. He said in the hospital that he had said a thousand times that there was no Christian, but he had to take it back. The dear Lord in His goodness allowed that man to see a man that was so saved that he could shout and praise the Lord and love him under the most intense suffering, and he may forget some things, but he will never forget working on the arms and legs of one little sanctified preacher. And he got so when he would come in to dress my arm he would say, "Bro. Bud, do you love me?" I told him yes, with all my heart and wanted him to go to heaven with me. He would smile and say, "I think that would be mighty nice." But finally my arm got so bad that he said one morning if he couldn't clean it up we would have to take it off, and by that time I was so bad I couldn't shout much. He went to work on the arm, but he seemed to be a little pale and nervous, and as he worked I prayed. I am sure it was not because he was at work on my arm that he was nervous or pale, because he was a great surgeon and operated on people every day, but the dear Lord had been talking to his heart. But as he worked on my arm and I prayed, little by little, the putrefaction seemed to pull away from the flesh, and finally when he got a great wad of it wadded up and lifted up out of the hole in my arm, he laid his tools down and said, "Glory to God, we have cleaned it up." He seemed to be so excited over it, that he rejoiced and didn't seem to know he was rejoicing. He probably doesn't know today why he said "Glory to God, we've cleaned it up and saved your arm," but the Lord knows that prayers were going up for him at that time all over the United States that he might handle my case in a successful way. For the readers will remember that when I was smashed up Brother Cornell wired *The Pentecostal Herald, The Herald of Holiness, The Christian Witness,* and *The Revivalist* asking the saints to pray for me and that God would undertake my case and that my life would be spared, and of course, with the readers of all these holiness papers which amount to multiplied thousands, when they went to prayer, God not only had me in hand, but had my doctor in hand, and that doctor was under the prayers and faith of probably a hundred thousand of the best people in the United States, and it is remarkable how God talked to his heart. There was one fine doctor, Dr. Gray, who assisted my surgeon, Dr. Rumwell, who was a member of the Presbyterian Church, and used to be a great friend to the Rev. J. O. McClurkan who is now in Glory. And when Dr. Gray found out that McClurkan and I had been personal friends for many years, he didn't charge me anything at all for his services, which was so kind and beautiful

MY HOSPITAL EXPERIENCE   23

of him. When my bills were settled there by the Rev. Donald J. Smith, who gave Doctor Rumwell the check, he said, "Almost, you persuade me to be a Christian," and he was so kind and beautiful on the last day that I was in the hospital. He came in the morning and dressed my wounds and told me I would stand the trip all right, and he asked me if I loved him, and I told him how good I loved him, and he went out and I supposed he wouldn't be back any more, but it wasn't long until he was back in my room again, smiling and looking so kind and pleasant and said to me again in a smiling way, "Brother Bud, do you love me good?" And I told him I did, with all my heart. He then went out and I supposed again that that was the last time I would see him, but it wasn't long until my doctor was back to see me again and smiled and said, "Brother Bud, you will stand the trip fine," but at the same time he asked me in his smiling way if I loved him, and I told him that I loved him and wanted him to go to heaven with me, and he smiled and said he thought it would be mighty nice. And while Dr. Rumwell was a great physician and surgeon, yet he had a place in his heart that was tender and he loved to be loved as well as the rest of us folks, and God had hold of his heart and was pulling him towards heaven. When he was going out of my room the last time, he wiped the tears from his eyes, and asked me if I loved him; I told him that I did and that I was expecting him to go to heaven, and I want to say right here, that if Dr. Rumwell isn't beautifully saved and if he doesn't make the landing in heaven, I am going to be the worst disappointed man there, for I just as truly expect the Lord to answer my prayers in behalf of that great doctor, as I expect Him to answer them when I pray for other people. And I know that God got him by the heart and gave him such a pull skyward that he will never get over it.

But finally the hour arrived for the ambulance to come for me and take me to the depot. We were to go down through the city of Frisco and cross the beautiful Oakland Bay, and there I was to board the train for Los Angeles, Calif. Bro. Donald J. Smith had bought tickets for my wife and me, and had secured a nice apartment, and when the ambulance men put me into their little trough, as I would call it, and lifted me up through the window and put me on my bed, it seemed to me that the Lord entered that train with me, and our little room for the night was full of the glory of God. We left Oakland at five o'clock in the afternoon and pulled into the city of Los Angeles the next morning at nine. While I was about four-fifths dead and one-fifth alive, yet the glory of God so filled my soul and filled that train that I literally shouted and praised God all night. I had one shouting spell that lasted sixteen hours, and it was five hundred miles long, and I will never forget how glorious it seemed to me as our train pulled up over the beautiful mountains some seventy-five miles north of Los Angeles. It seemed that I couldn't say Glory to God, and Hallelujah, and Praise the Lord, any longer, but I went down over the mountains and into the beautiful valley, and on into Los Angeles, with one whoop after another. While I couldn't say glory to God, I could whoop, and it was one whoop after another as we pulled into the

MY HOSPITAL EXPERIENCE 25

city, and when we arrived there was a splendid gentleman from Pasadena with his ambulance, Mr. Reynolds, and his driver. Little Sister Yarver had arranged with them to met my wife and me at the Southern Pacific depot in Los Angeles, and they were there to carry me across to my home in Pasadena. As they let me down through the window from our apartment, into the ambulance, I looked out, and saw a sea of faces, of my friends, and while they were praising the Lord and singing and clapping their hands, and waving handkerchiefs, I came down out of the train a whooping just as loud as I could whoop, and I went into the ambulance and every breath was a whoop. The young man that drove the ambulance was unsaved, and Sister Yarver sat out by him, and as I shouted across the beautiful hills between Los Angeles and Pasadena, she talked to him about his soul, and God got such a hold on his heart, that in a few days he was beautifully saved. And I expect to see him in heaven, and the reader can see at a glance that if I hadn't been smashed up he wouldn't have been there, and he would not have heard me shout, and Sister Yarver would have had no chance to talk to him, and he might have been lost. But thank the Lord, God can use the shouts of a man three-fourths dead to shout conviction on an ambulance driver. They finally landed me in my home, and my wife nad thought to keep me at our home, but I found out that I was unable to stay at home, and the only way I could live would be to go back to the hospital.

Arrangements were made for me to be taken to the **Pasadena Hospital**. **Room 202 was secured, and** on the evening of June 24th, my ambulance man landed me in the Pasadena Hospital. Dr. E. J. Matson had been secured to take charge of my case, and Miss Gray had been secured as my nurse. To talk about a kind nurse and a kind doctor, there is no way in this world to express their kindness and their love and their sympathy. As a nurse, Miss Gray is one of the finest that I have ever seen in my life, without it was the young lady who handled my case the first two weeks in San Francisco. These two nurses are the finest I have ever seen or known. I never expect to see them surpassed, for love and sympathy and kindness and ability. Dr. E. G. Matson worked on my arms daily for five months. Bless his heart, he never got out of patience, never gave the thing up, but held on to it with a death grip, and pulled out bones, and put on cotton and rubber bandages to beat anything I have ever seen. But he saved the arm, Glory to God. While my arm isn't as good as it once was, it beats none so badly that it seems to me it is a genuine, good one. But, in the Pasadena Hospital like it was in Frisco, I had no sooner landed than the beautiful flowers began to pour in, and through the long weary days of June, July and August, the great baskets and bouquets came in by day and by night. Another interesting thing about it all was, as my bills piled up from day to day, one of the strangest things I have ever seen, was how the money came in. The money literally came by the arm loads, I call it, and my bills not only run hundreds but multiplied hundreds of dollars, and while the doctor's bill would pile up, and the nurse bills, and room rents, and X-Ray bills and medicine bills, by the time they were

MY HOSPITAL EXPERIENCE

due, God had the money there to meet them. It came from all parts of the United States, from one dollar bills up to hundred dollar checks. And, every dollar was paid, and not only that, but while I lay and suffered, and God paid the bills, at the hospital, at the same time, the money came to pay all the bills at home, such as grocery bills, water bills, light bills, gas bills, phone bills, ice bills, besides all of the added expenses, as I was helpless for five months and a half. I want it known in heaven, and earth and hell, that God answered prayer, and not only provided for me, but for my family, much better than I would have been able to provide for myself and them if I had been in perfect health. And not only was my hospital and home bills settled, but other bills that I owed. God sent the money to pay them, and yet some people believe that the days of miracles are over. But to my mind, in my case, God worked as great a miracle as He did in the case of Lazarus, whom Jesus called out of the tomb. And I want to testify that during all these five months and a half that I lay on my back and suffered with my broken bones, and a sore back, and spent hours and hours so lonely, Jesus never left my bedside, and His presence was so real to me, that I could see His face on the wall. During all those months of suffering, I want it known in three worlds, bless God; that I never felt anger, or jealousy, or impatience, or revenge, or anything of the kind, get up in my heart. The man that smashed me to pieces never paid one dollar of my heavy expenses, and my heavenly Father is a witness to the fact that I loved him as I believe Jesus loved me when He hung on the cross. There was never a moment that I felt that he was doing wrong in not paying anything. It was left with God and with him. And the Lord had my case in hand, for I belong to Him, and God let the world know that He could allow me to be broken to pieces, and become as helpless as a baby and go through five months and a half of intense suffering, and that He could keep my heart so full of His love, that it seemed I was better off smashed than when I was not smashed. And I want the world to know that the visions I had of Jesus, and the answers to prayer, and the wonderful revelations I had of God and His love for me, were worth so much that it would have paid me to have had all my bones broken, because through my broken bones, God revealed Himself as I had never seen Him nor known Him before. In the darkness of the night God has written verses of Scripture out on the walls of my room until I could read them as though I was reading by the sunshine at twelve o'clock in the day, and to my mind that is one of the miracles that God wrought in my case. To some people it might seem strange that God would allow me to get smashed and then while I lay on my back in the dark hours of the night, throw beautiful Scripture verses on the wall for me to read. It would seem to them to be all uncalled for, but God does many things that the unspiritual mind would never understand nor comprehend. And another beautiful thing about it all is, God never has to explain to other people why He takes some of His servants through such hard places.

In praying one day, not long ago and talking to the Lord about my smash-up and suffering and why the Lord permitted this to happen, the Lord showed me

MY HOSPITAL EXPERIENCE 29

that I had been carrying a heart for three years that had been broken, in a way that the world would never understand the whys or wherefores, but God and the writer know all about it. The Lord showed me that it was through His goodness and love and mercy to me that He allowed my bones to be broken in order that while my bones were growing back, and my mind on them, that God also could heal a broken heart; and thank God, while my bones grew back, my heart also was gloriously healed, and today there is nothing but love for God and all of Adam's race in my heart. And though I had suffered at times as much in a week with a broken heart as I suffered in five months from broken bones, God's hand was over me, and under me, and His love so filled my soul that today I rejoice in the fact that God allowed this great fortune to come to me, that some people might call a "misfortune." For, as one of the poets has said long ago, "God moves in a mysterious way His wonders to perform; He plants His footstep on the sea, and rides upon the storm."

As I have just stated in the above paragraph that I suffered more sometimes in a week with a broken heart than I did in five months with broken bones, to a person that did not understand the dealings of the Lord with His servants, this statement might seem to be mysterious. Perhaps I can give you a practical illustration that will tell you what I mean, in a way that I could not explain the thing itself.

A traveler was passing through a beautiful country. The highway was perfectly lovely, and led through beautiful mountain scenery, and the beautiful springs were gushing from the hillside to refresh the weary traveler, and the murmuring brooks cheered his weary footsteps along the way and refreshed him as he slaked his thirst. The flowers were blooming along the wayside, the birds were singing, at times in his mind he could hear the beautiful songs that were sung by his wife and children and the shouting and frolicing of his grand-babies as they played in the yard, but as this traveler journeyed along this beautiful highway to the Celestial City, in the afternoon of life a dark stormy cloud rose over in the western horizon, that showed to the traveler that a storm was brewing. It wasn't long until the thunders were rolling, the lightning flashing, and the trees along the highway were uprooted. The clouds seemed to rise over the head of the traveler, and pass between him and the sun until the sunshine was completely obscured. Of course, while the storm was raging the birds were not singing, the flowers along the way seemed to droop their heads, and some of the trees that had been planted by gentle hands, were uprooted and blown by the road-side. At times the traveler could scarcely see the direction he was traveling; however, he had much to be thankful for, for he knew the City he was traveling to, and he knew he was on the road that led to that City. And while the storm was raging, the traveler became weary as he looked into the face of the black clouds, said some unkind things about the storm that was raging. He couldn't see at the time that it was all for his good, but after while the storm seemed to pass over and the sunshine once more broke through the clouds, and to the glad surprise of the traveler, he found he had made greater progress toward the City while the storm was on than

MY HOSPITAL EXPERIENCE 31

he had been making before the storm cloud arose, and then he apologized to the cloud and thunder and lightning, for even having an unkind feeling in his heart while the storm was raging so furiously. Today while the dark cloud still hangs out over the West, and so far as the traveler can see, may remain there, yet the traveler is making such progress toward the Celestial City, and the birds are singing so sweetly, the flowers are blooming so profusely and the murmuring of the brooks by day and night, is so entertaining to the traveler, that as far as he can see, the road clear through to the Celestial City is so bright, beautiful and glorious, that the traveler rejoices now over the fact, that his Heavenly Father allowed him to pass through a storm; the sun never seems to shine so brightly, as just after a thunder storm. And so it is with the traveler to the Celestial City; the devil may bring out a storm of abuse and misrepresentation until the traveler is peeled and scalded and blistered, and cussed and discussed and judged and misjudged, and treated and mistreated, understood and misunderstood, but Glory be to God, the Father, Son, and Holy Ghost, the way after the storm is more beautiful than ever before, and who would not be willing to go through a storm occasionally in order to come out and enjoy the sunshine and the singing of the birds. Well, amen, there is none but God can turn a stormy sea into a Haven of peace and rest. Bless His name forever!

The readers will remember that I have stated that while in San Francisco, Rev. Donald J. Smith handled the money matters and paid the bills, but when I reached Pasadena, Calif., the Rev. C. E. Cornell, who is my pastor, and also the pastor of the First Church of the Nazarene in Pasadena, Calif., took charge of my expenses, and raised hundreds of dollars and paid bills and handled my affairs with more love and patience and kindness than almost any man that I have ever known. And the Rev. A. O. Hendricks, of Los Angeles, and Bro. Cornell of Pasadena, are the two men on the Pacific Coast that the reader will remember stood by me when I was in heaven, and thank the Lord, they stood by me when I was on earth, with their love and sympathy and prayers, and their money, and their large congregations. Right here I want to thank the Lord for such friends as these two men. No man knows how much a friend is worth until he is so helpless that he can neither feed himself nor dress himself. Then he finds out what a true friend is worth. May the richest and choicest blessing of heaven rest upon everyone, and may the everlasting arms be beneath them, and may they be overshadowed with heaven. I promise all that I will stand true to the cause we love so much. Let me say in conclusion, that there is no power on earth apart from the sanctifying glory of God that can take a man through what I went through and keep him during all those months in perfect peace. I had thought that holiness was the greatest experience on earth and indeed it is beyond the comprehension of man, but I believe today that if possible, it is a thousand times greater and more beautiful than I had thought it was. I want to say, "Praise God from whom all blessings flow! Praise Him, all creatures here below, Praise Him above, ye Heavenly Hosts, Praise Father, Son, and Holy Ghost!"

www.ingramcontent.com/pod-product-compliance
Lightning Source LLC
Chambersburg PA
CBHW030313030426
42337CB00012B/695